I Love You, Call Me Back

Also by Sabrina Benaim

Depression & Other Magic Tricks

I Love You, Call Me Back

POEMS

Sabrina Benaim

PLUME

An imprint of Penguin Random House LLC
penguinrandomhouse.com

LIBRARY OF CONGRESS CATALOGING-IN-PUBLICATION DATA
has been applied for.

ISBN 9780593185872 (paperback)
ISBN 9780593185889 (ebook)

Printed in the United States of America
1st Printing

BOOK DESIGN BY ELKE SIGAL

for my mother, Santina

June 30

I dress in the dark. It does not matter if I forget my necklace or earrings. Keep forgetting which day of the week it is but remember to eat breakfast. Swallow the good white bullet that poisons the place where the lonely breeds. I am dancing again, in the kitchen, spicing sliced pears. I am baking again, in the restful yawn of morning. Each afternoon, I go for a walk through the cemetery, place pennies on the "Speller" graves. Sit in the grass cross-legged with the flowers and write a new religion, where we pray only *with* and never *to*. Read poems aloud and remember my favorite lines onto postcards I will procrastinate sending to the people I love. I live alone. Eight states and a border away from home. My cups are clean and upside down in the cupboard. I watercolor peonies instead of picking new wounds. When my tiny talk machine chirps, I do not always check it. I do not wish to see a ghost. I do not wish a summons. I allow myself to go entire days without speaking to anyone, except my mother. I swallow two bullets blue each night for the ever-grief. Sleep. I have not used the word *depressed* to describe myself outside of a poem in months, but I am drinking Diet Pepsi again. The thing is my head is a bright place I would not hesitate to invite you into. I've painted all the furniture marigold sunrise. Today, at 7-Eleven, I asked for a lighter and do you know what color the cashier gave me? Yes, keep me in this canary dream where I sugar scrub my lips soft as feathers and pretend to kiss. I confess, sometimes I cry when I look in a mirror, but I tell myself it is the mirror who is crying with jealousy. On the generous days, I tell myself I am sweet enough to spread on toast and call dessert. Then, I giggle, I am not afraid to feel silly. I am not afraid to feel anymore. You know, I wish I wasn't so sad, I have been in such a good mood. Want to know a secret? I think being in love is just a better kind of lonely.

“Dig.
Isn’t that what you’d say, Sabrina?”
—my mother

Aortic Aneurysm

Immediately I thought,

I've seen an episode of Grey's Anatomy *about this.*

I google :

aortic aneurysm / thoracic not abdominal / 5.6 cm / surgical procedures /

open repair vs. endovascular / stent vs. graft / risks / common complications

can you stop an aortic aneurysm from growing?

can you stop an aortic aneurysm from growing holistically?

what happens if a 5.6 cm thoracic aortic aneurysm ruptures?

why are all the aortic aneurysm statistics only documenting men?

statistics for the survival rate of women who just turned sixty last November with a 5.6 cm thoracic aortic aneurysm.

We hang up the phone.

I ask Siri,

> *Which season of* Grey's Anatomy *has the episode*
> *with the aortic aneurysm*
> *where the doctors did everything they could.*

Siri asks me to repeat myself.

I say,

> *I am not ready for my mother to die.*

Siri responds,

> *I don't understand the question.*

i put down my phone & binge watch
an entire season of a reality tv show.
ice cream for dinner & i'm dairy free.
for hours, nothing matters.

i water the plants out of habit, not care.
i watch the episode of *Grey's Anatomy*
which is about an aortic dissection,
not a boring aortic aneurysm.
this comforts me in the slightest,
but it could have been the ice cream,

or how my mom declared only four puffs of
a cigarette since the diagnosis.
she wants to live.
we will wait for tests to be done
to determine the appropriate procedure.

i see the colossal swell of depression
cresting over my day
& instead of holding my breath,
i wave to an old friend.

on video call,
i apologize for my splotchy skin
& my best friend tells me that i am beautiful
says that is the best thing about my face

Tomorrow Comes Anyway

My skin hurts
& I don't like my hair.
    Tomorrow comes anyway.
    The sun is not inspirational,
    it is on fire.
I have become
the queen of the uninspired.
I was once queen of the firebellies,
fell in love with everyone I met,
said nothing about my love,
let it grow & grow & grow until
the whole of it was gone.
    Like the moon.
    The moon is aspirational,
    it can be here & invisible.
I want you to know that
is almost exactly how I feel about myself.
I can be queen of disappearing from everywhere
except the mirror.
& it's easy to say a shadow is still a body.
    What exists cannot un-exist,
    only burn out,
    fall out of orbit.
My mind goes insane
& a body is a body,
even if I look at my body

& see a most misshapen thing.
My skin, it physically hurts,
	but I don't want to die,
	I just want to lie on the road
	for a little bit
while it rains & everything glistens.
Reigning queen of the glittering.
I rub my eyes with sparkles every day.
I want to see the world this way;
I want to look in the mirror,
reflect my shine back
	so blinding,
	I don't see anything
	at all.

i imagine diving into a bed of milk thistle & scratching
    my skin new.
i allow rotten thoughts like this to bloom like moon vine
    in the midnight hour.
i am ashamed.
i wish to exist as ladybug, fruit fly, small enough to hide
    inside of a tiger lily.

In a Text Message

the man I am in love with says to me,
"it's just that, in my head, you aren't real."

and like that, poof! I am a ghost. You once begged for a haunting. But you know what? Maybe some other time. Ha. Time is not real. I mean, I am more real than time. You are cruel. A kiss goodbye. A spell. Like the notes of a piano when you finger the right keys. Dancing in the living room, in your arms, you rolling up the sleeve of my T-shirt, wasn't I real enough? Perfect and temporary. A bloom curious about winter. A peach-colored rose called cinnamon. I fix myself a dinner of dandelion wishes; to be real to be real to be real. I sit on my yellow couch. Sing along with Mac when he says, *I think we just might be alright.* I will be alright. The rocks are aligned on the windowsill. The cutlery is asleep in the top drawer. Everything has its place. Your place is far from mine. Your face is far from mine. I think about missing you. I let it go. My hands do not shake when I remember I can barely remember how to dance in the dark. I buy a candle. I forgot my name, dyed my hair, sunset the song. It skips; my heart gallops away. Yes, I went and you stayed behind. And then you got mad and told me not to come back. But then you got mad when I didn't come back. And you didn't talk to me for months. And now you don't want to talk to me anymore. The first thing I do is forgive myself for how long it's taking to look in a mirror, touch my body and feel myself, better than perfect and good as any flower; I am real.

Escitalopram

Without you,
I move in slow motion.
Nauseous by midday.
To soothe,
I become a thick plume of smoke.
I flag surrender
        & depression takes me.

July 3

It is peculiar; the numb spell of
antidepressants. I wake up and repeat, and
repeat. Every day, in the park, with the birds
and their wing-flap rat-ta-tat takeoff. I only
dream of staying. But where? But how? I
use my fingernail to carve my initials
into the bark of the tree in the park, where
I sit for days, waiting to hear the wind's
voice. In the park, I am under the
impression the wind has forgotten
my name. Under a moonless sky,
counting cherry pits, I curse each star
for teaching me how to sit cross-legged
and burn. I must have died thirty deaths since
I last saw myself. In the park, the feeling
of wanting to say something true knits my teeth
together. I blink the minutes by, ask for wishes
from blinking streetlamps. The raccoons
drum a racket outside on the lids of
garbage bins, their noise another empty threat
of company. I do not care for sleep, unless
the dreams are of water towers painted with
my name. A whisper in the wind begs wait, or
perhaps the whisper is coming from
me. I want to believe the future is
a beautiful place. I reach for it, but my arms

Clonazepam

round	pill	to ease the panic
peach	coin	currency of calm breaths
compressed	zip file	of medicine
sugarless	rocket	disintegrates into dreams
swallowed	missile	to dissolve the quivering
& at once	a hug	a straitjacket

Aripiprazole

Each night my alarm rings 10 p.m.,
I bring my body,
perfect chandelier of teeth & bone,
to the altar of the bathroom sink.

I place two blue
berries of ripe motivation on my tongue
& swallow.

If it weren't for this,
I would do nothing but worry.

Imagine my mind,
a light switch,
this is the hand
that turns it bright each morning.

On Progress

during the video call the doctor asks about effectiveness

I bloom open each sunrise
wide as hibiscus petals

& what about side effects

the unbearable tightness of blue jeans

afterward, I sit at my desk & scroll through my camera roll
waste an hour comparing my body to its old figure

spiral into cans of aspartame bubbles & nothing else

burn the toast / toss it to the birds / do not make more

I cannot name all of the ways I have attempted to bend my bones

on the video call the therapist asks
when the disordered eating began

black bodysuit / pink tights / room of mirrors

& what do I love about myself here now today

as if the shiniest penny I might find
won't still be a penny

there are things I do because I know I am supposed to
things like leaving voicemails or salting the water when it boils

some days I cannot bring myself to think about chewing

if only I were fuchsia & flower
all I'd ever have to swallow is the sun

mom tells me her next doctor's appointment is in three weeks.
. . . three weeks.

Introduction to Santina

Scorpio
Red hair red lips & red nails to match
Black eyeliner & hairspray
Forever in heels
Walking disco song
Peacock confidence / Blows kisses to herself in the mirror
Grounded / Afraid of heights
Bad with directions
Social homebody
Thoughtful
Cries at commercials
Live, laugh, love enthusiast
Card shark
Dancing queen / White zinfandel, two-glass maximum
Loves to host a party
Loves knowing her neighbors
Loves a love story / a good love song
Favorite holiday: Christmas / Is Santa Claus
Is the sun
Relentless optimist
Has jokes
Will answer to Mama Bear

Mama Bear

She is waking me up for school.
Driving me to dance class.
Carrying the groceries in with both hands.
In the basement doing the laundry.
In her gray cleaning T-shirt.

Reading books aloud at bedtime.
Putting on elaborate shows to make us laugh.
Reading books with dramatic flair.
Helping with homework.
Taking me shopping for new clothes.
Doing my makeup for recitals.
Brushing knots out of my hair.

Making the bed alone.
Making dinner alone.
Baking dessert.

Sitting at the kitchen table
Ready to talk.

Buying me peach schnapps for prom.
My first box of condoms.
Scolding me for smoking pot in my bedroom.
Fighting with me about sleeping all day.

In the doctor's office waiting room.
The therapist's parking lot.
In line picking up my prescriptions.
FaceTiming me while I am crying.
Pulling laughter out of the dark days.

In the passenger seat telling me to slow down.
On the plane to celebrate my thirtieth birthday.
On the phone while I drive across the country.

Is there.
She has always been there.

The Good News

is spring still came.
Came anyway.
Hyacinths & strawberry
begonias bloomed.

Myrtle spilled over concrete corners,
those little lime green plants,
the ones that look like Shrek ears
sprouted into high-rise bushes.

The robins built nests.
Their perfect blue eggs
nuzzled in Desiree's mailbox.
I check on their well-being via Instagram.

I open the windows
to be a part of the world outside.
The world is outside,
yet is unfathomable.

I stay inside
repotting plants,
baking banana bread,
learning unnecessarily complicated TikTok dances.

I spend the early evenings wandering
the empty alleyways covered in fallen bubblegum petals.
I am talking about the flowers
because I miss touching you,

being touched by you,
being touched by anyone
who is not myself.
I am numb to the desperation

buzz of the *are you still watching* screen.
I want the sound of people talking
to fill my empty kitchen
while I wash my single dish & cup.

I have to keep reminding myself
an itch does not exist to be scratched.
I have to stop drafting
tweets composed solely of melodramatic lyrics.

To distract myself
I infuse honey with cardamom seeds,
practice French braids. I study

the robin occupying the tree
outside my living room window;
the robin sits & does nothing.
I mimic it for hours.

Daydream

I am your wife. You bring yellow flowers
every Monday when you arrive home.
I keep them out on the wooden table
no taller than a tulip standing
on the shoulders of another tulip.
We go for walks after the sun goes down,
steal daffodils from the neighbors' gardens.
All I want to talk about is loving you.
The wind rustles the rocks that hang on string
from the magnolia tree in our yard
like chimes, we waltz slippery in our socks.
We eat too many sour candies, but
live content in our little cavity.

most nights
we have a family-wide video call at 7 p.m.
i am watching my nephew laugh for the first time
through a screen

i am watching my mother watching my nephew laugh
everyone is beaming

July 5

Mabel wakes me up at 4:57 a.m.

Outside, it is quiet as a cemetery; nothing
but the sound of insects.
The feeling of not being good enough writhes inside of me.
Mabel doesn't care what I look like as long as I feed her,
play with her, keep her from getting bored, take her out,
and love her.
I do all of these things for myself and yet I cannot leave the house
without makeup. There is a voice in my head that paralyzes me.
I am surprised to find there is a safety under the mask of dusk.
Bare streets allow my bare face fresh air, a rarity.
Mabel & I are both relieved & for a moment
everything feels OK.
Back inside, I catch a glimpse of myself in the mirror
& begin to cry.

Poem Written from the Bath

my insecurities are rioting in the back of my head / they possess an urgency so startling / I am avoiding mirrors again / I am afraid to want anything / even the smallest crumb for dinner / feels like more than I deserve / so I am not eating / and then I am eating all of the time / I am terrified of what would happen if I missed a dose of medication / I set three alarms on my cellphone / wrote "TAKE YOUR PILLS" on a Post-it note and stuck it on the mirror so it blocks my face / look sometimes self-care is just surviving / though I've also been taking baths lately / cloud the water milky pink and scent it like a citrus grove / as long as the water obscures my frame I'm fine with baths / I like the time designated for just lying and thinking / though I have been over-thinking everything / like what if while in the tub I slunk my entire self below the surface and sang the saddest song I've got in the back of my head until all that was left was the soft hush of waves and not that piercing voice that says I don't deserve to be present / this is not about dying / I do not want to drown / that is not how I wish to go out / to go out is what I want / to leave the house confident is what I want / to feel like I can be looked at / to have the experience not make me want to apologize would be ideal / I feel like I am wearing my body / so I've been slipping into waters a little more opaque / pretend I'm lying naked and unashamed in the middle of that citrus grove / pretending I am worthy of the imaginary beauty around me / look / I think all I am trying to say / is I want the saddest song I've got / to stop being the only song I am capable of singing in tune i watch *Beauty and the Beast* to "get out of my head."

From Belle to the Beast

O, master of anger
I am your most loyal disciple

O, snarl & smile & sink, I
Sink to my stinging knees

O, you biting, silent beast
How you sulk & I accept

The challenge to lift you up
O, how I look up to you

Sensitive & stubborn statue
Of self-righteousness, you selfish decision

& yes, I do dream
Of having more than a collection

Of clipped claws & thistles
Pulled from my palms

O, how I beat myself soft
Scrub almost raw

You are the one coated in silken tendrils
We both know, you are the master

Because you need it
Because I let you

Because I want to earn your love
Because you won't give it to me

Any other way
O, how I wish I could

Be mad at anyone the way I am
With myself for not being mad at you

The Beast's Response

Look at all I have given you;
I built you a library,
And still,
You want a love poem.

Love Poem

I'm back in my favorite Friday night,
where the last thing he says to me
before falling asleep is *I love loving you.*

& I could not dream of anything sweeter,
so, I stay awake all night.

July 6

Once Upon a Time

Him : I will whisper I love you on my walk home.
Me : How will I know?
Him : I will whisper I love you until you hear it in the wind.

i take Mabel for a moonlit walk
without headphones
& as we turn the first corner
the wind catches chimes we cannot see
the jingle stills both of us
& i believe
i believe

Revival // Ode to the DM Slide

A midnight gesture
Surprise
Celebration
In blue light
There you were
Starry-eyed & yellow hearted
Honey
Cinnamon sugar / My mouth
watering / Song
Songbird / Hummingbird
Bone buzz
Electric guitar
Up the spine / Lightning
Bug / Burrowing
Under my skin / A harvest
Sweet as maple syrup snow
Weightless & playful
Delicious & unexpected
Undressed
I am iridescent / Offering of giggles
Abundance of tingling
Tambourines
& you / Charming thrill

You / Velvet mouth
Your mouth
I believe in the spell
Pretending to kiss
Come here
Come here
Come / Come
Come
Come here
Come
Come / Come here
You know
All I've ever wanted
Was for you to
Ask me
To dance

July 7

i haven't groomed my y'know since March
& even though i was born in 1987
i think i understand the seventies now
i put on "The Boss" by Diana Ross & twirl about

Addendum

I once told you my depression is a firefly.

The truth is:
I am the firefly.

If you pave a field of fireflies,
the fireflies will not migrate,
they will disappear.

My depression is concrete.

I am doing everything I can to survive.

The Red Dress

I am my mother's
November baby.
Her favorite daughter,
& her first.

The birds are loud
this morning.
While the phone rings,
I hum along.

She answers, *hold on*
making a coffee.
I take a sip of my own,
holding.

When she returns,
she begins. *So,*
I've been thinking
about my clothes.

Like, if I die,
you keep them.
The good stuff,
at the very least.

I am my mother's
only daughter.
There is no one else
to carry this.

Like my red dress,
tailor it, wear it.
I'm sorry, is this too much,
I was up all night

Thinking about that
stupid red dress
I kept for this long.
You should have it.

I am my mother's
preferred mirror.
When she looks at me,
she sees herself.

I tell her I will hold on
to the dress, the clothes,
the jewelry & teacups,
the Christmas decorations.

I tell her
I am hopeful
years will pass
before inheritance.

Okay that's good!
she laughs,
Good answer!
I sit on my hands

to keep them
from shaking.
& enough of that,
how are you?

I am my mother's
best student.
So I laugh. I laugh,
& I don't stop.

Whitney

Today, I went outside to have an interaction with a stranger to remind myself that I exist. This is how I know I am depressed again; I have to remind myself that I exist. I went to the plant store and the beautiful blonde girl behind the counter asked my name, and then followed it up by asking where I was from because she could tell I wasn't from *here*. She said she has a knack for being able to tell when someone is from out of town. So badly, I wanted to say *I'm still in the process of figuring out where I've come from, if you know what I mean*, but, instead I said, C*anada*. She was from Virginia, which she loves to tell people, because apparently being from Virginia is a very good thing. I'm glad to have left the house today to have learned that. I don't think I know anyone from Virginia, except Whitney at the plant store, who sold me a cactus which now sits on a shelf and every time I look at it I remember I am capable of going outside and telling a stranger my name. On the worst of days, I am still myself. I name the cactus Resilience. I do not touch its needles to prove anything. I am tired of relying on pain. Today I felt joy, because beautiful Whitney asked me my name. She also said she liked my hair, but I'm not trying to brag.

i am having cocktails with my friends
over an app we dislike but use anyway
for the bad trivia & good laughter
over whose neck wears the most wrinkles
or whose bookshelf is holding un-cracked spines
or worse—encyclopedias
i don't even notice the loneliness

afterward i finish the book of essays
that's been sleeping on my bedside table
i hang up a few Polaroids
slather blue clay all over my face
& soak in a tub of bergamot waters

before sinking into bed
i text my mother that i love her
i roll one sleeve of my black t-shirt up because i miss you

July 9

bird song / white noise / I blow a kiss to the robin I now refer to as *my* robin / I am so lonely / I'm beginning to like myself again / I am so sad / I forget the peaches & plums at the market when the wrong song shuffles up the wrong memory / the time my father told me depression turned me into a monster / but what a kind monster I can be / obsession is a loyal claw / not unlike the stuck hand of a stubborn clock / scratching away at the same moment / again & again / that time I told my father it was not the depression that made me a monster / I was only following in his footsteps / I walk home / soggy with nostalgia / at home I watch two episodes of a baking show while I eat a single roasted sweet potato for dinner / I fall asleep dreaming of golden choux-pastry / of getting the bake just right

On Hope

The father I hope my father to be has me by the ankles.
Hope is a brittle promise that someday things between us will get better.
If we're lucky he says.
But I know luck is a false saint the hopeful pray to.

I am heavy with hope. My father is trying to change.
I drag around this promise because hope is a stubborn dying.
What frustrates me about my father is also what frustrates me about myself.
I am trying to change.

I drag around this promise because hope is a stubborn dying.
Hope is a brittle promise that someday things between us will get better.
I am just like my father; I am trying to change.

I cut my hair to frame a boundary around my face.
I cut my nails to enforce the boundary.
I partake in a daily & weekly skincare routine & I do not skip steps.
Stay hydrated.

I am learning to help myself.
If I am lucky the lesson will stick for both of us.
But I know luck is a false saint the hopeful pray to,
& I know hope is a burden, an affliction.

I am trying to change. My father is trying to change.
& since *change* is a verb
today we spoke for thirty-six minutes.
I believe there is a future where I am not angry.

I hang up the phone feeling possible.
I believe there is a future where I am not angry.
A future where we are realistic with one another
& hope doesn't inevitably end in tears.

Ode to My Eyelashes

Rain collectors. Ever thirsty
beggars. Cupped & yet, reaching
fingers. How you are consistently
the first compliment I am given—
My what long & fluttering wings.
Oh, you waterlogged wings.
How the flight of each blink must
terrify you. How you hate to touch
your reflection. You prefer I keep
my eyes open. Sleep has taught you
to lie with your fears each night.
Oh, what sweaty & stubborn children
you can be. My immature, yet loyal
friends. How you stand at my attention
each morning, waiting for the brown,
muddy skies to wring out their rain.
Some weeks, drought. How it feels like
vacation for us both. While the weather
always returns, some of you leave &
never come back. I wish you well.
I am an abundance of tears & you are
my favorite bucket.

i cry from frustration more than any other feeling

the most successful way for me to stop myself from crying
is to distract myself

Ode to Sexting

I was asleep,
the way an instrument is asleep
when there are no hands or hot breath.

But you woke me,
taught me to play
a simple game where my hands were your hands.

& where there was silence,
inside of the empty room,
I became a song.

The Flowers, They Are Not Singing

I dreamt this up once long ago
& here it is:
a Sunday afternoon
spent falling in love with myself
if this is what it is to be alive
if this is all it is
Vampire Weekend parading
out the big white speakers
that, yes, I ordered on Amazon
forgive me but they make me feel good
they have this ability
to hook up to my record player
and sing to me
when I need the everlasting
arms of song the most
like this morning
after walking by the church
with Mabel
& swearing to God or Beyoncé
I do not need another body
even if
my honey arms refuse to hold love
only throw themselves in the air
in celebration of music
then "leave me to myself /

lead me to myself"
the music it's alive & so am I
sing sing sing
I did not die before I made it to thirty
sing sing sing
& toss my limbs in each direction
call it praying, dancing
I am crying
into the wind my propellers are making
I am watering the flowers
each tulip I picked
& potted
& strategically placed
around the apartment
to crowd myself with life
to prove it can bring me joy
& ask for nothing in return
I bow down
to thank the tulips
to thank the carnations
the marigolds & mini roses
thank the orange gerbera daisies
that sit on top
of the white speakers
sing sing sing
for today
the flowers
they are not singing
I am

on the front steps
smoking a skinny joint
i count the little joys of the day

drank plenty of water
went for a nice long walk
cooked myself dinner

in bed
Mabel stretches out along the side of my body
while i read a short story about colors

Ode to Purple Summer

I listen to the flowers. I hear them laughing. blooming, I mean. I take a bath in the kitchen sink. I pin myself to the map on the bedroom wall & look! Here I am, a nap on the cherry blossom carpet in the backyard. Instead of running circles inside my head, I go for a dance down the sidewalk. This morning, on the patio, I told the waitress, *I have my open-heart set on the smoked salmon hash*. I asked for coffee, she said, *and a water* with me, I did not say *jinx* out of respect. I dream of being coronated the king of ice cream sandwiches. I dream of having exactly enough change for the cashier. Sometimes waking up is like falling back asleep into my favorite dream. It rains, I forget there are clocks, sit on the stoop and read poetry. When the man calls me, he addresses *love* and I recognize he is talking to me. I recognize myself as love. I suppose this is what I am getting at, in the phone call, when I tell my mom, *I feel like I am living myself back alive.*

i am relearning desire, beginning with myself.

so, i slip into white lace & squander the evening
searching for the right light, photographing my body
capturing every curve in the full-length mirror.

We Mean the Same Thing

I wake up in a bed over a thousand miles away from my mother.
The sky is white and where she is, it is afternoon.
A plane goes by overhead, Mabel barks at the door.
A bouquet of now-
dried pink carnations sits by the window,
where I am talking to my mom
on the phone. She says she saw my tomatoes on Instagram,
suggests I give them to my neighbors, but no way
because I don't like them;
tomatoes or my neighbors, whose cat lies
a lazy king of the house, by the window,
Mabel barks and he hisses.
I'm sorry but forget about cat people, I joke, and we laugh, and
she slips in a *have you eaten* to which I reply,
two eggs on toast by 9 a.m.!

We both exhale. Far as we are, we have been walking side by side
on this journey to my becoming for thirty-one years.
The most important lesson my mother has taught me is
to never look up to her,
rather, to look beside myself, and there she is.

Voicemail from My Mother

Sabrina,
One more thing.
There's an old gray bathrobe,
Slung in the back of my closet,
If I die,
I want you to come straight here
& empty its pockets.
There should be enough money
To get you through the first few weeks.
& if I make it through
It's a family vacation.
I just want you to know
I'm thinking of everything
So you won't have to.
I know you're worrying
Even though you don't tell me.
You can tell me.
I'm still here.
I love you,
Call me back.

the first time he told me he loved me,
i told him i was so happy i could die.

& he said
go ahead.
& i will breathe life into you, little ghost.

The Un-Fairy Tale

My swallow has returned.

The box sits in the mail
like this bird

who refuses to leave
the nest it has made
of me, a feathered creature

my mind must have mistook for kin.
Fluttering fear that can't fly.
Wings kept on the inside.

Kind of like this madness.
This flightless fury.

I hope the mail
stays undelivered.

I do not wish
to have my belongings back.

Keep my heart.
I don't want it.

I've got this swallowed panic.

This bird
keeping me up at night.

I do not need a heart.

I do not need anything else
alive inside my chest.

On Anger

at birth a butterfly was placed in the center of my palm
    & instilled in me was the instinct never to make a fist.

my whole life, sun open hands, because I was told
    the butterfly would stay, until I gave it permission to leave.

but why would I release my most tender feature?
    the butterfly that has saved me so many arguments.

see, I built myself a chair to sit in when my blood
    threatens to curl my fingers inward one by one.

my chair is so uncomfortable, it distracts my hands,
    pulls me back into my body & I can let it go.

I'm good at letting anger go in the moment but I will hold
    a grudge.

I've come to love my butterfly enough to feel anger,
    not to let it consume me, this means avoid it.

but that is the lesson of the butterfly is it not?
    to avoid destruction at all costs. to hurt no thing, no one.

after the conversation where I told my father to go to hell,
    he did not speak to me for eight months.

you know it was my father who placed the butterfly in my palm.
do you think he knew then he would be the one

to deliver & deliver & deliver me to the doorstep of a tightening fist?
was the butterfly's intention all along to shame my rage?

I read on twitter someone's therapist said *your anger knows*
you deserve to be treated well and with kindness.

your anger is a part of you that loves you. then how come
for me anger is as useful as holding my breath?

i wish to be anonymous or brand-new
i want everything you know about me to be wrong

i waste the afternoon
teaching myself to play
"Dream a Little Dream of Me"
on the children's keyboard
i bought last summer

Dream a Little Dream of Me

night breezes
    sing
        a   dream

            and me

  me   me   me

    I'm a   blue
        little
star

    craving

        longing to

            sunbeam

all

whatever

of me.

July 15–19

Return to the Slow Now

I wake up
I go back to sleep

draped in soft morning glory
I return to the spot / in the park
not where we lay / but where we
lie still / entirely in love
& I am

I wake up on the couch
I move to the bed

we are eating dinner / on the sidewalk
one plate / one beer / two glasses / I pour
you ask me to take off my sunglasses
I look at you / again for the first time
& I am so relieved

I wake up with socks on
I turn off the lights

at the bar / votive candles
branches of lilac / hand holding
across the table / when we pay
the bartender calls us a cute couple
& we are

I wake up to wash my face
I change from pants into shorts

a bouquet of orange at the airport
the welcoming of a lifetime / coming
home to you / the yellow table
& I wish for nothing but this

I wake up
I go back to sleep

Aubade with Ladybird

5:13 a.m.
pink sky
pink moon
pink carnations
in the vase
on the table
beside my bowl
of waiting green grapes

I haven't been
touched
in months

//

pink
streaming
through
bamboo blinds
the plants a pollock
of light & shadows

a ladybird lands
on a ruffled petal
& catches my gaze

if I were a bell
I would ring
high & sad

if I were
a spoon
I would be
for salt

//

windows cracked
the wind conducts
the leaves
to accompany
the chirps & whistles
promising the blue sky
coming

this month
every morning
is the same

//

empty bowl
means coffee
I sit on the steps
sip slow

as the steam
or the sun
prompts my eyes
to close

what would it take
to be slipped on
like soft pink
satin light

what would it take
to exchange
these sunbeams
for fingers
hands
flesh
against my flesh

//

6:52 a.m.
come back
inside
to find the ladybird
gone
Mabel is awake
ready to be walked
& fed
errands are to be run

to the bank
the post office

slow dance
the memories
back to sleep

one year ago
every day of June
I woke up crying

//

today
I woke up
alone
lonely
& still in love

I touched myself
in the shower
to the thought
of you

The Extinction of Honey

While walking toward you,
for what was the last time,
I came across a swarm of bees

in the middle of an intersection.
I stood in awe of the buzzing,
honey spilled from my eyes.

I knew it could not last,
this sweetness between us,
it was always going to sting.

meanwhile i'm hungry
but not going to eat
smoke instead probably
maybe snack
gotta switch my laundry
washer to dryer
i could say *bad morning*
& mean
i woke up
not in love again
plus it's only 10:53 a.m.
so i vacuum the stairs
take out the recycling
drink a coffee on the steps
listen to a podcast
fit the sheets to the bed
collect the littered bottles

of hand sanitizer
& arrange them by the door
my stomach growls
i scroll twitter for the news
the day's death count
my anxiety needs to know
to remind me
to be prepared
people die
at any given moment
people get sick
get in car accidents
mothers get 5.6 cm aortic aneurysms
that could spontaneously burst
i wash the dishes
dry the dishes
wipe counters down
maybe i am going to eat
boil a pot of water for oatmeal
salt the water when it boils
because i know i am supposed to
when i think about my mother dying
i know i am supposed to
distract myself with a physical act
like cooking or cleaning
& as of late
my house is spotless

Panic Attack

I don't want my mother to die. I don't want my mother to die.
I don't want my mother to die. I don't want my mother to die.
I don't want my mother to die. I don't want my mother to die.
I don't want my mother to die. I don't want my mother to die.
I don't want my mother to die. I don't want my mother to die.
I don't want my mother to die. I don't want my mother to die.
I don't want my mother to die. I don't want my mother to die.
I don't want my mother to die. I don't want my mother to die.
I don't want my mother to die. I don't want my mother to die.
I don't want my mother to die. I don't want my mother to die.
I don't want my mother to die. I don't want my mother to die.
I don't want my mother to die. I don't want my mother to die.
I don't want my mother to die. I don't want my mother to die.
I don't want my mother to die. I don't want my mother to die.
I don't want my mother to die. I don't want my mother to die.
I don't want my mother to die. I don't want my mother to die.
I don't want my mother to die. I don't want my mother to die.
I don't want my mother to die. I don't want my mother to die.
I don't want my mother to die. I don't want my mother to die.
I don't want my mother to die. I don't want my mother to die.
I don't want my mother to die. I don't want my mother to die.
I don't want my mother to die. I don't want my mother to die.
I don't want my mother to die. I don't want my mother to die.
I don't want my mother to die. I don't want my mother to die.
I don't want my mother to die. I don't want my mother to die.
I don't want my mother to die. I don't want my mother to die.

Shane

He picks up & says he is so excited
to see my name on the screen.

It is 2 a.m. I am having a panic attack.
The tears are streaming, I am sitting

on the curb. Fresh air is not helping. I am sobbing
outside, sweating in an oversized sweatshirt

but Shane answered the phone. Immediately,
he tells me that he loves me before asking what's wrong.

I tell him I can't stop crying.
I tell him I need him to just talk.

He launches into a story about the date he is still on,
& I start laughing not because the story is funny,

but because Shane picked up my call on a date at 2 a.m.
& is now telling me that I am not a burden

over & over while I insist he go back to "dancing"
& he insists he has not stopped "dancing"

so it's really no problem. He knows I need to hear it
& his love is unselfish, always making sure

I get what I need. It's so easy to love him back
in exactly the same way. Shane is my best friend,

& he has been for twenty-one years.
Shane is my best friend

because he refuses to end the call
until I rap a song lyric & prove to him that I am okay.

I take a deep breath & without thinking, sing,
until, until there is no longer, let's get lost inside the clouds.

He laughs, *alright, okay.* We say I love you
at the same time before hanging up the phone.

July 21

My heart is a wound.
Healing inhales an eighth a day,
or buys another oversized T-shirt dress,
while swallowing sugar, calling it medicine.

Healing inhales an eighth a day.
Shame is an old friend of mine.
I swallow sugar and call it medicine.
Use indulgence as self-care.

Shame is an old friend of mine
who taught me how to make an excuse,
to use indulgence as self-care:
it's always acceptable to buy a new dress.

Let me teach you how to make an excuse;
when pampering oneself, be comfortable.
It's always acceptable to buy a new dress.
The dress is a Band-Aid.

When pampering myself, to be comfortable,
I bought an oversized black T-shirt dress.
The dress is a Band-Aid,
my heart is the wound.

Dream a Little Dream of Me (Reprise)

I

miss me

while I'm alone

i daydream a dream of clear skin
& dig into my imperfections
until my nails are painted red
& makeup proves me believable
when i say i have been doing well
& all my mother knows
is what she sees & likes on Instagram

Selfie

The sky is a photograph,
I do not take it,

because every moment moves on or dies and we are left foolish for attempting to remember while foolishly forgetting the last thing we spoke into the wind before we hung up our tongues or fell asleep or simply stopped talking it's so early in the morning I am sitting on a yellow couch I am calling home but no one is awake to answer & now I am thinking about you that morning you woke up and I was sitting in your kitchen that morning I woke up and my kitchen was your kitchen too I think about you this morning making coffee in some kitchen and no matter what color I picture the walls I am wrong and envious of the mug warm and lucky in your hands & yes yes I do still dream of your arms but now they are columns of roses cut at the head

I kiss my clean teeth together to form a smile,
& in the photograph I take of myself,
I look happy.

In the Spirit of Being Real

Too close to the house we once lived in I now live the promise of a future you broke with both eyes open don't say you love her I can tell by the photographs the future is a promise I made with both eyes shut I woke up became a ghost to you please don't say you love her I can tell by the photographs it is just how you wanted you are happy you are I am running or else stuck standing still crying about it every room I walk into I paint the walls gray call it cloud frequency devour the blue make heavy what is a memory if not another rock in my pocket I collect many small things make heavy spend my days hung upside down heavy call the sun the moon but don't use the word *depressed* I wouldn't use the word *depressed* a flightless shadow aren't I floating above my own head a scrap piece of paper push-pinned to the wall it reads I wish to be with you I do not read it aloud I trace it with my finger into the wind do you re-member the names of our imaginary dogs? they bark in the mornings I have recurring daydreams of orange flowers in airports I am picked up by no one when I arrive unannounced quiet as a yawn in an empty house I live with the echo of who I was I walk by the yellow house the green water tower I offer a truce I walk home in the opposite direction of the house we fucked on the wooden floors of the house that housed a snapshot of what could have been forever & wasn't & just so you know I can tell by the photographs her pockets are light she can give away a smile without a worry for the cost of making it & I get it I do paper beats rock & now heavy I am heavy I am so so

Alternate Reality

I don't know you.

*

I still work at Starbucks
Still pray for my period
Or would if I were getting any.
    (I make a note to bring up in therapy
    why in my self-imagined alternate reality
    I'm still not getting any)

*

Someone is laughing in the home of everyone I love.
In some cases, it's the person I love.
In some cases, it's someone else who loves them.

*

A stranger smiles at me but I miss it.
I'm too busy looking down,
looking at my phone,
scrolling for a reason to smile.

*

My father comes back, and I forget how to cry.

*

My full notebooks empty themselves.

*

No one hears the poem.
My mouth stays a moon full of silence.

*

I've never cut my hair short.
I wear it in a long side braid.

*

I don't know you.

*

While walking Mabel
we run into a giant husky
and when its human exclaims,
"She's so small!"
I politely ask her not to say so too loud
"She doesn't know," I whisper.

*

The pages on the calendar of the years I was loved but left
untouched fall out.

*

When I order pad thai medium & it comes spicy, I enjoy it.

*

When the man at the gas station blows me a kiss while I pump
gas, I pretend to catch it.

*

I've never googled "aortic aneurysm."

*

I don't take baths for fear of shrinking.

*

I paint my nails the same soft lilac every time.

*

I dream of wide-open space.

*

I don't know you.

my nostalgia hardly sleeps
i sweep it sweetly
under my clinical sadness
call it sweet-pea
because it keeps me up till dawn

July 23

On Your Birthday

rise before the grapefruit sun to leftover pie & too hot coffee & press play on my most recent playlist & antidepressants birth control mood stabilizer glass of good room-temperature water & feed Mabel take Mabel outside check the mail knowing there is none & while I believe in telling the people you love that you love them I do not send a happy birthday but because I also believe in abracadabra I sing along with the song that says I & love & you & look I know it's over but dizzy the nostalgia & I'm positive I wasn't the only one who glimpsed a photograph of our could-be future that night we lay down on someone else's driveway counting falling pine cones & kissing & I remember every note to the spontaneous song of your fitful laughter when the magician appeared & it was just like that time our eyes met in the mirrored tent that night we both whispered secrets beneath the neon lights & giant green water tower & it's only 2 p.m. here & now I slip into my clean bed & close my eyes tight to take a break from missing you & make a wish to blow out every candle I have lit to bring you back when all of a sudden a memory appears & unwraps itself before me it's the voice of the petite brunette at the café show in Portland who found me crying after my set & said *all the love you've ever felt still lives inside of you* & she was right & she is right & it's time I regift that love to myself

Poem from the Bed

Imagine a bed.

I imagine a medium-soft bed with at least two pillows and
a comforter; a fluffy comforter,
not heavy like gravity, but there is a decent weight to it
and it is cool to the touch.

I imagine the bed is in a room and the windows are open.

On the windowsill, there is—I imagine; a candle, melted,
three-quarters of the way down its jar,
two pine cones sitting in the scoops of wooden spoons,
and a small gold bell.

I imagine if I pick up the bell and ring it
you can hear it from wherever you are.

I imagine I am too afraid to ring it even once.

There is a calendar on the wall still set to March, a record player
spinning *Sinatra at the Sands*, there is nobody in my room but me.

Once a week, on Sundays, I pick exactly three flowers and put
them in the clay vase I made at camp one summer that sits on my desk.

I imagine that balmy camp air and it is not better than the air
here, in my room, with my bed.

I say out loud the things I need to remember; vet appointment
Monday at noon, therapy Tuesday at one-thirty,
I don't have to feel sorry for choosing myself.

It is here where things get complicated, real.

Because I have imagined a bed, I want to lie in it.

Truth be told, I am not sorry for choosing myself, just lonely.

I imagine I am the kind of person who is okay with that.

self-care

oversized t-shirt & black bike shorts uniform

i've been pressing on nails because they are dull
& don't draw blood

The Wedding Ring Speaks

sat in the jewelry box   for eighteen years   until her
    twenty-fifth birthday
when her mother   plucked me   a ripe carrot from the
    garden
        & presented me to her

I returned to a finger   even the middle
    I fit perfect   shameless in refracting light

she loved me   just as she had as a baby
I was   surprised to find in her
my reflection

seven years   she was faithful to me   took me off
only to bake   & then (of course)   forgot to put me back on
(a few days)   I forgive her absent mind

having vowed to never marry
    I am her longest standing commitment

this could have been a sad story
    I could have told you about the end   the affair
the girl's own panicked trembling   but none of it matters

when dawn's first light finds me
    on her hand   as it glides cobalt across the page
each morning I sing

I came from love
I came from love

& would you believe
this morning
    the girl sang along

calamitous is hope
still i cradle it in both hands

Who Needs Music

once my father told me
if I want a person to fall in love with me
I should never sing in front of them
& once I heard a crush say
"she has a terrible voice" to a mutual friend
& I knew my father was right

I spend a quiet hour deadheading
the campanulas on my desk
listening to the birds outside
with their long coos & long tails
I look for the robin
& it is there on the phone line watching me

in the shower I sing
you're the only friend I need
to Mabel through the cellophane curtain
she stares back looking unimpressed
today I find myself singing
while the blender makes my lunch smoothie

I sing loud as I can
I've never felt more alone
& sometimes it's easy to be depressed

& in a good mood
to be lonely
to parade my loneliness around in my underwear

at the top of my lungs
that will never be enough
I think I could be enough
enough is temporary
& so am I
so I am enough

Voicemail Left on My Mother's Answering Machine

Mama Bear
where are you?
are you okay?
could you call me back
immediately?
I'm sorry
you're probably fine
probably making a sandwich
or
on the house phone
or
reading to the baby
or
outside in the backyard
maybe
repotting the mint
maybe
in the laundry room
maybe
I'm sure you're fine
I'm overreacting
but do call me back
immediately
please

sorry
I love you
okay
I love you
call me back

In the last memory
I have of my mother
I am looking up to her
Shivering
The same fever from yesterday
I am sitting atop her feet
My limbs twist tied around her ankles
To keep her warm.
The next morning I woke up
& became my own mother.

My grandmother told me this story
years ago
& I remember being devastated.
"Not even a goodbye?" I asked.

Just gone in the night while I dreamt.

i have many vivid dreams

in all of them
my mother is alive

A Certain Uncertainty

My mother's aneurysm
 is a balloon named
uncertainty.
 It is the opposite
of a wound,
 but brings the same
grief.
 Despite this balloon,
I have to believe
 my mother will live
to see many haircuts
 & birthday Sundays.
I do not imagine her
laying herself down
on a cold steel table.
 I cannot envision
the reality
 that our future holds.

The doctors say
 they will monitor her.
In the new year,
 another CT scan,
measure the aneurysm,
 maybe surgery then.

My mother exhales
says *this is good news,*
it gives us Christmas,
we'll worry next year.

I mimic her relief,
inside of me,
uncertainty
swarms, settles, slow
like dust,
thick, heavy dust.

Excerpt from This Morning's Phone Call

Mom,
are we going to talk about what will happen
if the aneurysm bursts?

Did I tell you we got a new printer?
The thing was such a pain to set up.
It wouldn't print a single page
until we figured out we had to have the computer
forget the old printer.
We aren't the only ones with memories you know.
Which reminds me, did you get that check in the mail
& did you get your new parking pass
& how was therapy the other day?

It was thrilling.
She asked me how lonely I am
on a scale of one to ten
& I cried instead of answering.

Well I'm sure that was cathartic.

It was fantastic.
I also told her you are avoiding talking about the aneurysm.

I'm not avoiding anything.
Did you see that video I sent
of your nephew walking?
You didn't respond to it.
Did you see how fast he goes now?

He was almost running as fast as you are
away from this conversation.

Sabrina. Please.
I don't want to think about it.
Everything will be fine.

(& it is here I realize her fear is more important than my own &
if something horrible were to happen before she goes into
surgery, or during surgery, only her body knows
how it will react, & it won't tell. it can't tell.
she literally can't talk about it.)

I'm sorry.
What are you making for dinner?

Oh!
Did I not tell you about the roasted cauliflower recipe?
I made it last week & we are all obsessed over here.
You've got to try it.
Let me write it down & text it to you.
Tell me what you think.

That sounds delicious, Mom.
I have a cauliflower in the fridge.
I'll make it before it goes bad.
Before it's too late.
I promise.

i rub the entire cauliflower with olive oil & a mix of
sea salt, black pepper, garlic power, & paprika
bake it at 450 for about twenty minutes
i squeeze a little lemon juice on it

before eating i text my mother a photograph of my plate
she responds with a thumbs-up emoji followed by a heart

On Video Call with Chim

We are talking about how much we love
airports. Overpriced coffee, sitting on the floor

because that's where the available outlet is, listening
to the playlist made for that specific trip.

Being at the airport brings out the obnoxiously nice side
of me, I tell Chim. I smile at everyone, especially children

who have their own mini rolling bags. I go out of my way
to make sure I say *thank you I hope you have a wonderful day*

To the attendant who sells me a bag of trail mix
& the eight-dollar green juice I will forget is in my backpack

Until the following morning when I wake up jet-lagged
& have it for breakfast. Chim laughs, wow, we are the same.

It has been 223 days since I have been in an airport.
More, since I have been patted down, strip searched,

if you know what I mean, I tell her & watch her jaw go slack
on the screen. I make a joke about owning a lot of batteries.

Chim shakes her head, cracking up, I hate you, she declares.
I say, yeah, but you at least find me desirable right? & she says,

wait, are you serious? & I think I am serious, but instead I say, nah, I know if I were a sunflower seed I would be honey roasted.

Chim doubles down, now I really hate you, but also, promise me next time you are in an airport it is because you are coming to see me.

July 26

last night I had this dream
where I was calling you on a landline telephone
one of those old ones with the rotary dial
I was calling you & it was ringing
& ringing & I knew you weren't going to pick up
but then you did & you said *goodbye*
& I said *thank you* & you said *I'm sorry*
& I said *I know but I don't forgive you*
& you said *then why did you call?* & I hung up
& when I woke I recounted it in writing furiously
afraid to lose even the mirage of you again
it is true that I don't forgive you
but I would consider giving up every good
& glowing memory I hold of us to make one new one
where we are sitting face-to-face across a table
or side by side on a park bench or lying down
in the grass but probably we would be walking
& I would be too afraid of making eye contact
knowing the moment I really looked at you
I would hear Bruce Springsteen singing to me
you can't start a fire without your little world falling apart
& I would be rushed with urges to destroy
this world I'm building without you
where I eat the tomatoes I grow
& *lonely* is a word I use to describe single socks
pulled from the laundry & not my heart
which is lonely but I prefer not to name that
I call no one & have a conversation

with the robin outside of my living room window
here every room I walk into is a living room
in the yard the flowers wear crowns of butterflies
I crown myself queen of dreaming
of you
& then queen of waking up

the house
four houses to the left of me
put a sign in their garden

it reads :

Have You Heard It

& yes
for a long time
i heard it

i try not to listen to the wind anymore

Maddie Texts Me to Look at the Moon

& so I go outside but I cannot see the moon from my stoop / so / I slip back in, slip on shoes, Mabel's collar & before I know it we are in the park / by the empty basketball court / where the light is / Mabel searches for the right patch of grass / & I am looking for the moon / that neon cantaloupe / that cold scoop of vanilla ice cream / I walk past the park to the 7-Eleven / looking for the moon made me hungry / I buy a pack of almonds, a can of Diet Pepsi / take a complicated way back / weave through the side streets to tire Mabel out before bed / back home I pop the tab on the can / once Mabel is curled up asleep on the yellow couch / I sneak out onto the stoop / with each sip I tell myself a secret / *I have not eaten anything today / I do not even want the almonds / buying them is enough for me / I am always distracting myself from the root of the problem / I would rather be hungry than lonely* / I look up but then I remember I can't see the moon from my stoop / only the stars / only the dead, dull stars / I go back inside / I eat the almonds while I watch a rerun of *Law & Order* / & when the bell inside of me rings / in my notebook, I write : *could not see the moon at all tonight / bring up eating in therapy / text Maddie—thank her, tell her the moon was exactly the reminder I needed.*

July 27

I step inside of myself & find an orchard
of pears fallen upon the unforgiving ground.

I cannot find one offering a fresh bite.

Below the sliver of lopsided moon,
inside of me, there is a great lake.

Its waves rush the sound of my little laughter in the cold air.
I lift a seashell & hear myself crying on my birthday.

Everything I keep inside of me has already happened.

I reach & toss my one & only stone into the great lake,
it boomerangs back into my pocket.

Heavy it sits.

I step outside of myself & find it is another Monday night.
This year every season asks the same question.

I answer the same ordered noodles, run a bath,
smother my skin in a mask so green

I am reminded that spring is still a winter away.
How many ugly ways have I tried to clear the blemish of
    loneliness:

eat or don't, sleep or don't, cry or don't, move or don't—
    loneliness.
My quiet house. My rotten pears.

I soak in waters warm enough to forget the weather,
I light a candle, two, fill the room.
Say a prayer for snow this November,

which is surely an offering as beautiful as fruit in May.
& perhaps I have always been the snow & the pear tree.

& my one & only stone, not a stone,
but a seed; my heart.

Heavy inside me it sits.

& nothing's gonna change.

July 28

i'm on my morning walk
just walking
listening to music & a lyric
mentions a color
the next thing i see
is a flower of that color

i'm walking
& when the beat drops
a bird or butterfly swoops
into my line of vision

i used to think
these synchronicities
were evidence of magic
these days
i'm just grateful
for the time & space
to notice them

it is still summer
swelter
fan on

i wear the same
pair of black bike shorts
i work on my monthly playlist
i watch old episodes of *Grey's Anatomy*
keep my house clean as a scalpel

i am present
sitting at my desk
watching the clouds move
calling it writing

i am present
when it rains
i cry along
collect the droplets in glass jars
& water my plants

everything is growing
my string of hearts sweeping the floor
my hair
long enough to pull into a low ponytail

this urge inside of me
to stop dining on dandelion wishes
to stop tossing all my bread to the birds
to go home

yes
i will miss the robin
no
i will not miss wearing Band-Aids on my face to bed
like i am now

i miss myself confident

i need to bring myself to my mother
to her altar dressed in red
i need to lay immersed in her boundless optimism

i need to believe in miracles
once again

i practice my winged eyeliner skills
i look nothing like myself
i kind of like it

Song of Rediscovering Myself

Dead June bugs & full, clear moonlight
dance in my house, on my living room rug,
while Frank oceans a pink sky
through the speakers, a new dream glows,
silly quiet. Just below the ceiling,
my frizzy, frizzy hair sits a warm fire
next to you; Sweet myrtle in bloom!
Pink magnolias! Honeysuckle! Swoon
like a shooting star wish—a hand
reaches in my direction & I believe
in its mouth, that day moon lullaby.
How lovely the air by the open window
my finger traces initials carved into
a wooden table, there was always
a girl before, a cold winter.
Me, I am an impatient thaw.
Be it in a park, graveyard, or coffee shop,
I decide it is here I am my favorite self,
& so what, if I read too many books
at once. If I never finish my last beer
fishing for a sunrise. So what if I can't stop
talking about that night & the three-piece band
in the bookstore, after hours. How
every time the door opened, a solo tear
from the trumpet snuck off into the night.
I want you to know, that night, I was
the final tear to fall. Took the long way

home to walk by the lilac tree, to whisper
you are so very lovely up into its arms
& *it's okay to ache lonely past midnight*
it said back. & I can't say I don't taste
my loneliness, clear as champagne.
All I've ever wanted was to come home
to a spoonful of honey, asleep in a soft bed
while a cool breeze from the ceiling fan
stirs our exhales together & then up
into the room, where I fall asleep
& do not dream of dying, though I do believe
I will recognize my death like some gorgeous
orange & purple sunrise I've already seen.
Instead, I will dream my hands
into lazy giants, napping by a willow tree.
I want to mean it when I say I can let go.
Pull the pine cones I have been collecting
from my pockets, shake the last of the dead
bees from my hair. All of a sudden the grass
is green again. Y'know, it rained on the first
day of summer but it was so weird
all I heard was laughter. & I don't know
if I believe in God, but I have cried
in every kind of weather. I cut my hair
& it always grows back. I am so alive,
my bones are always buzzing :
you are here you are here you are here.
I am the only neon sign I'll ever need.

Voicemail from My Mother

Sabrina
I'm sure you're still asleep
I wanted to call anyway
I was just thinking
I love you
I can't imagine anything but the best
For you
For both of us
Okay
Don't you worry
We're both going to be just fine
Know it
Believe it
Also call your grandparents
It's their anniversary
Okay
I love you
Around the world & back again
Sweet dreams
& good morning

July 29

today is my grandparents' sixty-third wedding anniversary
i can't even commit to drinking a glass of water
before my first coffee

My Mother Wrote This Poem Using Lines from My Poems & Calls It: An Imagined Day in the Life of Sabrina

I go out into the world
A walk
& it was no thing
Patio weather

My chin up
& I talk to myself
I am the party

The warmth of a smile
Remembering
But I look forward

& gently into the evening
I like to get high
When the full moon howls
I howl back

The truth is
I laugh

I am not afraid of the dark
For a better look at the stars
There are never enough

Sweet home
There is a stillness now

Looked in the mirror & thought
Look at you
I love you
I said
I love you

& if it weren't for my mother I wouldn't know how
& I am grateful for that

In Praise of Tomorrow

Jon says, today we are going to write a poem of praise. Say praise & all I see is my mother's face. It's going to be hard to write a poem praising my mother because she may die & a montage of all the good feels like something that happens only at the end. I do not want this to be the end. My eyes beg to spill even now at the sight of my scribbles recalling the time she stood outside of the bathroom door generously giving me a tampon tutorial because I refused to let her in. I cannot think about the time I called her on Interstate 81 & had to tell her I had just run over a bear & would you believe she laughed, said, *oh, that's my daughter alright.* & I am her daughter. Everything good about me I've either inherited or learned from her. So praise my stubborn & praise my loyal. Praise the cookies my mother insists we bake each Christmas. She tells me she wants me to continue making them when she is gone. I tell her she doesn't have to say things like that, I have crafted my heart after her sentimental kingdom. I still drink from the plastic Burger King cups I used as a child. I will make the cookies. Because her mother made the cookies. Because her mother made the cookies. I praise them all for passing down these recipes for patience. I would not know anything of its virtue if it were not for that rubbery dough refusing to hold the shape of an S. My mother's name begins with S & so does mine. Praise S for the sadness that swims in my marrow. S for the silent treatment my mother gives when she's mad. Praise we are not perfect & that is why we remember to be kind. I cannot imagine existing without her but the reality of the situation we are in has made me all too aware that I will have to someday. She says she doesn't want to say even a practice goodbye before the surgery. Says it's too hard to bring up all the good things without crying & there is no reason to spend any of the time we have left together crying. So, I do not say goodbye. Not even when we hang up the phone. I say see you later. I say see you soon. & *see you soon* she sings back, in praise of tomorrow.

i want the day to lay itself down

let me lie down beside it & dry like a small bundle of lavender
preserve me like this—saying words because i like how they feel :

velvet / velvet   parachute   moonbeam / moonbeam /
moonbeam   mother   alive / alive

July 30

A Dream // A Memory

I can hear Mac Miller whispering from the clouds because we are speeding in Pennsylvania / where I once ran over a dead bear / & now that seems like some kind of metaphor / like I have learned a thing or two since then / because of that / I am a good driver / the entire bear incident wasn't even my fault / but is another story / here I have only alive & pulsing offerings / take this citrus fruit & fine white sugar / almost a full tank of gas / memories still developing like Polaroids facedown on the dashboard / my friends are here & they are glad to be / I am so glad for that / for this night / clear enough to see the stars / not that I am even looking for a sign / I am watching the mile markers fall back faster than the beat of this song / it's easy to forget that we will all be gone someday / when we are so present in the right now / Shane is driving & dancing & hitting all the ad-libs that are & are not there in the song / Clementine is chilling in the back seat / & I am / a bop along / a giggling bop / all nodding / all yes / there was once a king who whipped it down the same stretch of 76 / probably / we smoke a blunt in his honor / in the hotel room / overlooking the yellow metal bridge / & then we go on sharing the good word through art / through these gospels / while holding hands with our anti-depressants / singing psalms in the key of thrive / I think whatever keeps you moving forward might be the same thing keeping you alive / & on this night in Pittsburgh / we are living as if everything is love in our ears / & all we need is lit up before us / a freeway & a bright night sky / holding us down

On Uncertainty

& then my therapist said,
sometimes the best thing about tomorrow is
we don't know what it could bring
I thought the best thing about tomorrow was its relentless arrival

& yes, I do know nothing is certain,
but watch me pluck daisy after daisy
ask question after question.
There are never answers, only probability.
My mother's aneurysm is probably a result of years of smoking.

The only thing we think we know for sure is the past,
but our memories are stories we tell ourselves to sleep at night.

I had a tumor once, in the middle of my throat,
it was the size of my pinky finger, about 5.6 cm in diameter.
The doctors could not conclude why the tumor grew.
It didn't matter, they made a perfect plan to remove it.
& they did, barely left a scar.

Our bodies are unreliable machines.

The doctors can't make a plan for my mother
until they run more tests:
to see how strong her heart is

how strong her kidneys are
can't know for sure how her organs will handle surgery
which method of repair holds lesser complications: stent or graft.

Possibilities arrive by the bouquet.
Knowing what could happen
but not knowing if it will happen
is torture.

My mother's aneurysm could sleep until surgery
be clipped & my mother returned to optimal health.

Or,

my mother's aneurysm could burst & kill her
before she ever makes it into surgery.

I want to cry & cry.
I want my mother to live forever.

& yes, I do know the closest thing we have to forever is right now,
but I also know the sun will rise.

So I make a to-do list & title it tomorrow,
& the first thing I write is to call my mother.

To-Do List

Call your mother.

Make the bed.

Have coffee on the steps & listen to ~~the wind~~
the robin's song.

Mail the postcards you have written.

Eat the half avocado in the fridge.

To soften the sting of being untouched,
add things to your carts online.
Do not purchase anything.

Spend an hour reading.

Laundry.

Grocery store:
oat milk
bananas
cantaloupe
cauliflower
sweet potatoes

Remember the day can be unspectacular & still a success.

Cry if you need to.
Dance when you can.

Instead of looking in the mirror,
look to the flowers & find yourself.

Here you are, in this endless golden hour,
in bloom, open & open & opening more.

Even if it is the only thing in this world you are sure of,
pull your name from your lips & sing.

THANK YOU THANK YOU THANK YOU

Paige / Suzanne / Bhavna / Marya / Everyone at Doubleday & Plume

Aeman / Jon / Desiree / Chim / Mac / Jess / Devin / Gume / Bill / Clementine

the good news crew / emotional historians / undercurrent babes / awful good writers / slumbies

Mom / Tony / Jesse / Spins / Forrest / Dad / Nanny / Papa / Meme / all my family members

Shane / Emma / Matt / Mike / Arjun / Jill / Nora / Greg / Wendy / Holly / Steph / Smit / Natalie / Katherine / Maddie / Mandee / Rachel / Phil / Mabel / Ryan

Every poet I've read / Every poet I've worked with / Every poet I'm lucky enough to call friend

& You / & You / & You / & You / & You / & You / & You / & You / & You / & You / & You

& since there are thirty-one days in July, here are thirty-one people, places, & things I was grateful for while writing this book : *Animal Crossing: New Horizons* / mini cans of Diet Pepsi / Tena

ASMR / MSIKU White Wedding / Origins Clear Improvement face mask / Portland, OR / Glossier Generation G lipstick in Like / bunny ears cactus / the Internet / Mac Miller / LOOP juices / Discovery Walks / Earl Grey ice cream / smoky quartz / press-on nails / baths / blue Flow Writer pens by Typo / flowers / gray T-shirts / reality TV / @urbangardenerto / Alberta Park / AirPods / tamales / Toronto, ON / Vans / peach Perrier / Moleskine note-books / the Postal Service & its workers / my yellow couch / coffee

About the Author

Sabrina Benaim is a poet, storyteller, and workshop facilitator. She is one of the most-viewed spoken word poets of all time: her videos have reached more than one hundred million people. In 2017, her debut collection, *Depression & Other Magic Tricks*, was a Goodreads Choice Awards finalist, finishing just behind Rupi Kaur's *The Sun and Her Flowers*. In 2020, she took part in the Heavy Hitters Festival alongside Ani DiFranco, Amber Tamblyn, and Mary Lambert. She lives in Toronto, Canada.